Henry Ford was born in 1863 in Michigan, America. He lived on a farm with his five brothers and sisters. Everyone expected Henry to become a farmer too, but Henry was not interested in farming.

Henry Ford

Instead, Henry liked to see how things were made and what made them go. He would sit in his bedroom and take things apart.

clock

He liked to take apart anything with a mechanism, such as things from the kitchen, things from the farm, and even his brothers' and sisters' toys!

When Henry was sixteen, he went to Detroit. Detroit was very big and lots of things were made there. Henry had to walk nine miles to get to Detroit and he lived there for three years.

Detroit

In that time, he became very interested in a new mechanical thing called a motor car.

Motor cars had only just been invented. If you wanted to travel somewhere, you had to walk or go by horse or, possibly, go by steam train or boat. Motor cars were very, very expensive and only the very rich could afford one.

motor car

In 1888, Henry married a girl called Clara. Clara lived on a farm not far from Henry's family. Henry and Clara set up home in Detroit and soon had a boy, whom they named Edsel.

Henry still dreamed about motor cars and planned to build his own one day.

Henry started to build his car. He built it in his shed at home. It took him a long time.

When he had finished, Henry was very pleased with the car, but when he tried to test-drive it, there was a problem.

As he tried to drive his car outside, he found that it was too big for the shed doors. So, to get it out of the shed, Henry knocked a hole in the walls.

Henry started to make cars to sell. They were all made by hand, which took a long time. They were very expensive and still only the very rich could afford them. Henry wanted to make a car that everyone could afford.

So Henry started to make different sorts of cars. Instead of calling them names, he gave each sort, or model, a different letter.

In 1908, he sold his first Model T Ford. It cost 825 dollars, which was very cheap for a car at that time. Now it was not only the very rich who could afford a car.

Model T

The Model T Ford was given the nickname of the "Tin Lizzie", and everyone wanted a Tin Lizzie.

Henry could sell cars that cost so little because he had found a new way to build them.

Before, cars had been made one at a time by a team of men. This took a long time.

Henry Ford set up the first "assembly line". Each man made only one little bit of the car. The car would then go on to the next man in the line, who would do a different bit. The car would continue along the line until everything was fitted onto it.

assembly line

Henry's new assembly line meant that cars could be made more quickly and more cheaply than before.

The men did not need to know how to build a whole car. They only needed to know how to build their little bit of it.

factory

Henry built a big factory at Highland Park in Michigan. He paid his men well and tried to treat them well. In return, he wanted them to be good and stay out of trouble.

Edsel Ford helped his dad to make the cars and then to run the factory. At first, all was well and Henry Ford became a very rich man. But other factories started to use assembly lines, and all cars became cheaper.

Edsel

Henry and Edsel had to try hard to keep the factory going. Edsel Ford died when he was only forty-nine.

Before there were lots of cars, there were very few roads. As more cars were made, more roads were needed so that the cars could drive along smoothly. No one wanted to be rattled around in a car as it drove across bumpy tracks. More and more roads were built for the cars to drive on.

If there were no cars, you would have to walk to school and back. You would have to carry your shopping home. Just try and think what your life would be like without cars!